BENETTO
FORMULA 1

Chris Bennett

with Maurice Hamilton

OSPREY
AUTOMOTIVE

To the mechanics, the unsung heroes

First published in 1994 by Osprey, an imprint of Reed Consumer Books Limited, Michelin House, 81 Fulham Road, London SW3 6RB and Auckland, Melbourne, Singapore and Toronto

ISBN 1 85532 421 0

Editor Shaun Barrington
Page Design by Paul Kime/Ward Peacock Partnership
Printed in Hong Kong
Produced by Mandarin Offset

ACKNOWLEDGEMENTS

During the past four years or so my involvement in photography has permitted me both to experience and participate in things that 'civilians' rarely can. When the suggestion to produce a 'behind-the-scenes' book dedicated to a front running Formula One team was accepted, I must admit that the prospect was actually both exciting and daunting.

It is fortunate that I joined forces with Benetton-Ford. Renowned for their positive attitude and openness, once the initial familiarisation period was over, it was a relief to find everyone within Benetton both positive and helpful. I am most grateful to them for taking this visiting stranger under their wing.

In a photographic volume such as this, cooperation is vital – if I don't get access, I don't get pictures – it's as simple as that. As far as the team were concerned the access was there, and it is my fervent hope that they feel the result – an informal, pictorial portrait of Benetton-Ford in action – justifies my presence within the exclusive domain of Formula One motor racing.

It certainly *has* been a very enjoyable experience, living up to my expectations in every way, and then some. It has also been a rare privilege to work with such a fine team of dedicated professionals.

Without calling the register it would be impossible to name everyone who helped, directly or indirectly, in the production of this book. And then I'd still end up missing someone out. Therefore, you'll just have to accept a beer at some point, preferably when I can afford it! I would however like to express heartfelt thanks to: Flavio Briatore, Tom Walkinshaw, Michael Schumacher, Riccardo Patrese, Ross Brawn, Rory Byrne, Gordon Message, Joan Villadelprat, Frank Dernie, Mick Ainsley-Cowlishaw and Rod Vickery. Thanks also to Willi Weber, Katja Heim of KH Promotions, Barry Griffin and his ever cheerful Goodyear team, Steve Madincea and Xavier Crespin of Ford, Allan McNish, Martin Whitaker, Mike Vogt of TAG Heuer, John Pitchforth of Nikon UK, Paul Waller of Commercial Cameras, Woking, Jon Woods and Stuart Nicol of Sporting Types, Stephen Tee, Charlotte Hare (for the open line to Silverstone), Anna Hobbs, Maddie Phelps of Silverstone Circuit, Sophie Ashley-Carter of Travel Places and Di and Stu Spires for feeding and sheltering me. Finally, a very special thank you must go to Patrizia Spinelli of Benetton – without her help this project wouldn't have been possible.

For a catalogue of all books published by Osprey Automotive please write to:

The Marketing Department, Reed Consumer Books, 1st Floor, Michelin House, 81 Fulham Road, London SW3 6RB

ABOUT THE AUTHOR

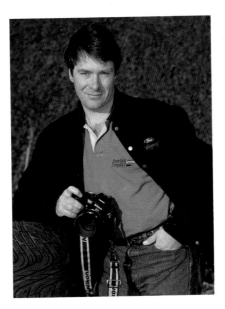

BENETTON FORMULA 1 is the fifth book that Chris Bennett has produced for Osprey. His first two works featured military aviation subjects involving F-15 Eagle and F-18 Hornet jet-fighters in Germany. His third and fourth books were pictorial tributes to the ubiquitous Land Rover and outrageous Lamborghini Countach. Currently he is working on a number of future books: on the Range Rover, AC Cobra, and a further Formula 1 volume. In addition to books, the author submits material to various car magazines. Chris Bennett is also involved in fashion photography – the two on occasion combining to advantage. All images reproduced within this volume were shot exclusively with Nikon F4S cameras, fitted with Nikkor lenses and loaded with Fuji Velvia RVP and RDP film stocks.

Maurice Hamilton has been writing on motor sport since the early 1970s. For ten years he edited the *Autocourse* Grand Prix annual. He has been Motor Racing Correspondent for the *The Guardian, The Independent*, and currently *The Observer*. He is Grand Prix Editor for *Racer* magazine in the US. Amongst other awards, in 1987 he won the Timo Makinen Award for outstanding motor sport coverage, and is a regular Formula 1 BBC radio commentator.

Commentary
by Maurice Hamilton

What you see on television is but a fraction of the story. The Grand Prix driver is the sport's high-flying ambassador; the star of the show. But he is, in effect, pressing the throttle on behalf of a multi-million dollar industry.

Behind the scenes are the unsung heroes. Beneath the surface is the most advanced automotive technology in the world. The motivation for all of this is a relentless passion for being the best; for competing at the highest level; for winning races.

Grand Prix racing is a fast-moving glamour game where the stakes are high and the rewards plentiful. But the commitment required is as breath-taking and dynamic as the show itself. Benetton Formula is a leader in this elite band of Formula 1 performers.

Sixteen times a year, Grand Prix racing sets out its stall in places as diverse as a former wartime airfield in Northamptonshire, the immaculate streets of Monte Carlo and a technically challenging road course in Japan. But, again, that is only part of the story.

Time in between is spent in a tireless search for perfection. From the moment the first lines of the Formula 1 car are sketched out, a multi-talented, highly-skilled business moves into action. From the model makers to the aerodynamicists, from the engineers to the mechanics bolting the first car together, every tiny detail is examined and optimised.

Then comes the shake-down trial on the track, the opening barrage of information from the telemetry on the car, the initial reactions of the driver, the first of many debriefs as the technicians begin to assess the potential of their product. Talking, sifting, calculating, debating, estimating, gambling, rationalising.

And, all the while, wondering what their rivals are up to. Are they doing it better? Have they found some secret ingredient? Will they be faster and more successful? Who will earn the television coverage? Who will ultimately score the most points and win the World Championship?

The debate is the same within the boardrooms of the dozen or so teams prepared each year to subject themselves to this public examination of their capabilities.

Allan McNish, Benetton Formula's test driver blasts into the daylight at Silverstone, to contribute to the team's insatiable appetite for perfection and knowledge

Above

In an icy cold Silverstone garage Riccardo Patrese, fresh from partnering Nigel Mansell at Williams, looks on as his car is prepared. The United Colors of Benetton's initial involvement with Formula One was in 1983 as sponsor of Tyrrell. A two year programme followed in 1984/85 to back Alfa Romeo. However by 1986, Benetton had decided to increase their participation in the sport dramatically and, to that end bought the Witney-based Toleman team. Benetton Formula was established and a future force to be reckoned with was born

Right

Riccardo is strapped in and ready to roll, as the Ford Cosworth boys make final pre-start checks to the valuable 'HB' engine. Since acquiring Toleman, Benetton drivers have achieved seven race victories plus a considerable number of podium finishes. The completion of their new, purpose-built factory in 1992, signalled clearly to all Benetton Formula's serious intention to become a major force in Grand Prix racing

Above

Michael and his trusty technicians prove that the outwardly serious business of racing does have its lighter moments...

Left

... and he takes Jonathan's hint about Mickey Mouse lap times in the right spirit. Michael claimed his first Grand Prix victory at Spa Francorchamps in 1992 and a well deserved second win at Estoril in '93

Some will possess an immediate advantage because they have more money. But some will spend it more wisely than others. Grand Prix racing has always been like that and will never change. It is the application of talent from drawing office to race track which really matters. The driver is the focus of attention. But everyone plays their part. It is a thrilling team game par excellence.

At Benetton Formula, there are 175 people working with the single aim of getting one of their cars across the finishing line first. The purpose-built 85,000 sq. ft. headquarters at Enstone in Oxfordshire is typical of the modern racing facility which only the top teams can afford to possess and utilise to the maximum. The overwhelming impression is of spaciousness, efficiency and cleanliness. And a burning desire to win.

Since proving his outstanding natural talent for motor racing, 'Schuey', as he's affectionately known within the fraternity, commands national celebrity status in Germany and consequently he's in great demand by both media and advertising. Here Michael's personality comes across as he takes part in a TV commercial, also ensuring that the team's sponsors get a look in too

The technical office, headed by Ross Brawn, is dominated by computer screens, the magic of the microchip allowing instant visions of components which would otherwise take hours to reproduce on the traditional drawing board. Once finalised in detail on screen, the information is transferred direct to the production department and fed into the manufacturing machine. Intricate components materialise with scarcely the need for human intervention.

The chassis , or 'tub' as it is known, is made from mixtures of carbon fibre, Kevlar and Nomex honeycomb. Numerous layers of this composite material are united at carefully calculated angles to ensure that the tub has the stiffness and strength necessary to carry enormous stresses while affording the driver a high level of protection.

The tub is moulded into an aerodynamic shape and then 'cooked' in a giant oven known as an autoclave. But, before the car can be completed, stringent crash tests must be carried out on the tub before the car is permitted to take part in a race. And these tests are severe, taxing the engineers to the full as they search for maximum performance while paying due heed to the necessary demand for driver safety. Ultimately, the chassis must be stiff, light and of course capable of withstanding a massive impact.

Left

Attired in Camel-sponsored racesuit, Allan McNish, Benetton's able test pilot, considers the task ahead. The constant demands for testing are such that Benetton have an independent test team, complete with driver, mechanics and transportation etc. Although a lot of the more important, decision-making sessions are performed by Michael and Riccardo, the third crew help to relieve some pressure from them and their mechanics. For McNish the post of test driver provides an excellent opportunity to gain valuable experience in an FI car

Below

Cocooned by the BI93B's carbon fibre cockpit, Michael waits patiently as Cosworth's telemetry systems come on line. Particularly during the off-season winter months, Benetton's local Silverstone circuit often has inclement weather. Consequently the team frequently pack their bags and commute to places like Estoril or Imola, where the odds are rather more in favour of good conditions. If it is too cold or wet, testing can prove a wasted effort. Systems under review often perform unrealistically, and in cold weather tyres may well not reach their normal operating temperatures, possibly leading to the acquisition of inaccurate data

Above

Apart from being an exceptional racing driver, Michael Schumacher possesses two other vital qualities – the ability to analyse what is happening to the car on the track, and – as important – how to communicate this information effectively to the engineers, so that consequent modifications can be made. Such abilities are essential in a driver if the car's potential is to be quickly maximised

The hope is, of course, that the latter requirement will not be put to an unplanned test. But from the moment the car rolls onto the track and the preliminary checks have been carried out, the engineers expect the driver to quickly begin exploring the car's limits.

The routine of testing is tedious and time-consuming but the results pay huge dividends. Benetton is not alone in employing a driver purely for this purpose; often a young driver who is a prospective candidate for Grand Prix racing in the future but needs to gain the experience in a Formula 1 car while completing anything up to a Grand Prix distance in a day – perhaps three or four days running.

But a lot of the test driver's time is spent hanging around while adjustments are made, new ideas tried and then measured against the stop watch. The improvement might be worth a mere tenth of a second over a three-mile lap. But, in the intensely competitive world of F1, that's progress. The blink of an eye can cover several cars on the grid when the serious business begins.

The build-up to the season gathers momentum a couple of weeks before the teams are due to leave for the first race. The new car will be

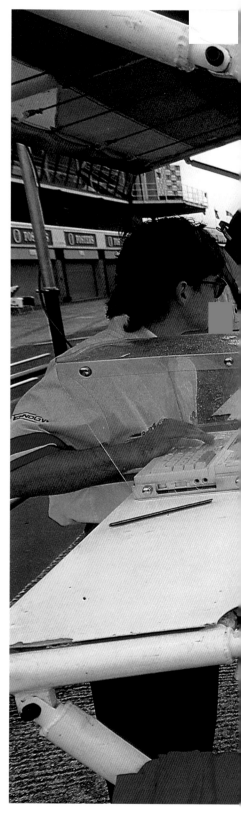

Above

Michael signals for his engine to be fired up as the electrically heated tyre blankets are removed. Track time at Silverstone doesn't come cheap and the efficient test team ensure that very little of it is wasted

Right

The crew look on as Schumacher smokes his tyres in a standing start acceleration test of the new traction control system. One of the so called 'drivers aids' to be banned in '94, computer operated traction control senses when the rear drive wheels lose grip and attempt to spin under power. Engine power output is then automatically reduced accordingly. This in theory permits the maximum amount of torque to be transmitted to the track for optimum acceleration, regardless of conditions. The traction control system's degree of effectiveness can be regulated by the driver

officially launched – perhaps in the business-like surroundings of a race track before a test session, or in the function room of a major hotel, or at the factory itself – and this will be a chance for the cameras to focus on the team colours, often bearing allegiance to a new sponsor (as was the case of course for Benetton in 1994). The drivers, naturally, will be centre stage. It is frequently the case that at least one will be new to the team but both will appear slightly self-conscious as they parade their latest overalls, stiff with newness and the insignia of the companies investing in the team.

There will be speeches, words of encouragement, talk of winning races and the championship. The proceedings will be upbeat and full of hope. Last year is history. It all starts again in a couple of weeks. Who can stop us now?

Although timing of laps is now accomplished by state-of-the-art electronics, Chief Engineer Frank Dernie still likes to involve his trusty stop watch. Frank is an acclaimed engineer and aerodynamicist and, prior to joining forces with the United Colors, worked for Williams, Lotus and French based Ligier

That almost euphoric sense of occasion is put into sharp perspective by the intensity of race weekend. Much of it is a matter of well-rehearsed routine. But the carefully orchestrated pattern of events has a single aim; winning. It's the same in every team even though, for some, success is but a fleeting hope. At Benetton Formula, anything less than victory is unacceptable.

That principle applies whether it is Sao Paulo or Silverstone, Monaco or Montreal. It's just that the method may vary to suit the widely differing circumstances. The long-haul races – South America, Canada, Japan and Australia – are known as 'fly-away' events because every single nut and bolt must be boxed and flown rather than loaded on the team's transporters for shipment by road.

These pantechnicons, two to each team, serve the races in Europe. The responsibility for their £1m cargoes is onerous and yet the team management, drivers and mechanics will expect to find everything in place when they arrive, ready for action, from the local airport.

The working conditions at the majority of permanent circuits have improved beyond measure. Gone is the varied assortment of garages and

Above

The 'T-car' or spare, receives attention from the capable hands of Paul Seaby. Three cars are taken to each Grand Prix – the two race cars plus a spare. On at least two occasions the team have been very thankful for that well prepared T-car. At Hockenheim Michael had last minute problems with his own car and, switching to the spare, drove it to second place on the podium. Later at Estoril, he was to claim Benetton-Ford's only '93 win, also using the spare car

Right

Schumacher hurtles up the gradient towards Coppice, in one of his familiar exhibitions of uncompromising race craft, during qualifying for the European Grand Prix at Donington Park

lock-ups, each track now required to provide pits and facilities which must be to a standard size with adequate supplies of light, power, compressed air and running water.

It will take the truck crews a full day to unload the transporters and set up the garages, complete with mobile tool chests, equipment and, of course, the three cars (one for each driver, plus a spare). Not wishing to waste a single opportunity to show the sponsors' logos, the trucks will be washed down and the garages decorated with tailormade banners which will form a backdrop to his scene of intense activity during the next three days.

The one exception is Monaco. Because of the temporary nature and

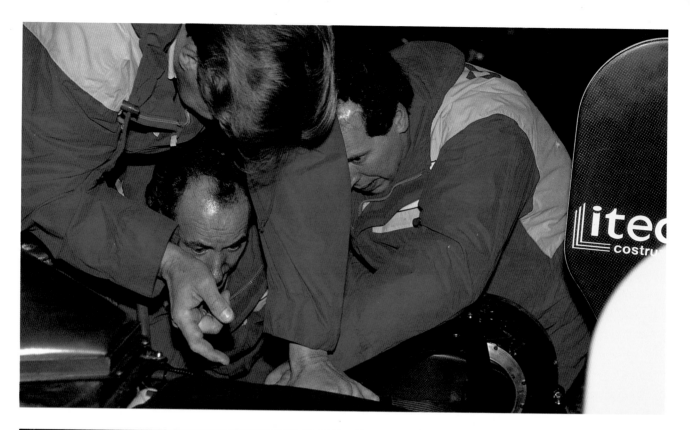

Above left
The Benetton scrum. Team-work is the essence of Formula One and the highly experienced mechanics each have their own primary tasks and areas of expertise. Often these jobs have to be performed against the clock, under pressure and the ability to stay both calm and level headed are essential requirements of the industry

Left
Only uncompromising perfectionists need apply for a position at Benetton Formula. Carl Gibson gives the 'BENETTON SPORTSYSTEM' decal that final finishing touch

Above
Kenny Handkammer checks the fitting of a front air deflector. Kenny's primary area of responsibility is the gearbox and rear suspension on Schumacher's car. Prior to joining Benetton five years ago, he gained valuable racing experience with an F3000 team

cramped conditions inherent with this street circuit, the paddock is some distance from the pits, the mechanics working under awnings slung from the transporters parked on the quayside.

This is the one lingering throw-back to the days when garages did not exist and the pits were exactly that; usually a grubby brick-built shelter boasting a counter but barely enough room for a handful of personnel. Cars were either worked on in the pit lane itself or returned, via gates at the end of the pit road, to the paddock. The convenience of today's adequately appointed garages fronting onto the pit lane, the transporters parked by the rear doors, makes the facilities of 20 years ago seem archaic.

Grand Prix racing has moved on in every respect. The technicians and engineers notice it more than most. Their role is dictated by computer software and printouts. Gone are the days when adjustments to the car would be based totally on the hunch of the driver and an educated guess by the man earnestly making notes on his clipboard.

Above
During a lapse in the torrential rain, Michael joins his boss Flavio Briatore, Managing Director of Benetton Formula, on the pit wall

Left
In the midst of April showers at Donington, Michael prepares to navigate the Melbourne Hairpin. The weather was a mix of good and bad, the race itself being very wet indeed. Not a particularly good time to be a trackside photographer – the novelty and glamour of FI can wear off! The European GP saw the maiden outing of the B193B, Benetton's '93 challenger. Whereas the B193A was a passive '92 spec car fitted with active suspension, the completely new 'B' had been conceived as an active car with improved aerodynamics

That continues to apply to a certain extent but the conclusions these days are reached with the aid of graphs and statistics. It seems that everything capable of being measured is monitored; lap times, segments of lap times, maximum speeds at various points, acceleration and deceleration, g-forces, temperatures, throttle openings, brake applications, steering inputs. Simply checking tyre pressures in the time-honoured way now seems old-fashioned.

The lap time is the ultimate arbiter. There can be no excuses on either side. TAG-Heuer, manufacturers of precision sports watches, brings more than 100 containers of equipment and 16 technicians to

Above

The European, which went from wet to dry to wet again, wasn't to be a good Grand Prix for the German. He had qualified an excellent third on the grid, behind the Williams' of Prost and Hill, but unfortunately failed to finish, spinning out on lap 22. Riccardo, who had started from a lowly tenth, did however complete the race in fifth position, following four tyre stops

Left

Jon Harriss washes brake dust off the wheels and tyres. Jon has two areas of responsibility – driving one of the big Scania trucks to the races, and once there, looking after the tyres of Michael's car

each race. Olivetti takes care of the data processing and each lap by each driver is recorded instantly by three separate timing systems. The information is displayed instantaneously on monitor screens. It is here that the driver receives black and white confirmation of his progress. Or lack of it.

During practice sessions, the facts and figures are discussed by the driver and his engineer by means of radio communication, the driver pushing a button on the steering wheel, a microphone built into his crash helmet picking up his comments. To anyone watching from the sidelines, it seems like some deaf and dumb routine as the driver waves his hands; the engineer, staring down at the cockpit, nodding and then moving his lips.

And, all the while in the background, the furious sound of activity as

Above

Time proven design methods are combined purposefully with advanced CAD/CAM (Computer Aided Design / Manufacture), in Benetton's ceaseless quest for progress. In excess of 170 people are employed by the team. All have to be totally dedicated professionals and no matter whether involved in design, engineering or PR, all are acknowledged experts in their respective fields

Left

Welcome to Whiteways Technical Centre. This unpretentious name is given to Benetton Formula's new £12 million factory complex and headquarters located at Enstone, Oxfordshire. Occupying a 10,000 sq metre site, the spacious, purpose built facility houses some of the most advanced research, development and engineering technology available, and is designed to focus Benetton's challenge for the world championship over the coming seasons

cars scream past the pits, lap times changing constantly on the monitors, everyone looking for that illusive tenth of a second. They know it's in there somewhere. Finding it can often be infuriating and sometimes impossible.

Once a conclusion has been reached and a decision is made to try a subtle change to the set-up, the engineer passes his instruction by radio to the mechanics working on that car. Not much needs to be said since changes will follow a number of familiar courses; adjustments to wing angles, changes of springs and dampers, alterations to wheel settings, adjustments to brakes and their cooling ducts. Perhaps a new set of tyres.

The tyres are the responsibility of two mechanics, one for each car. It is they who trolley the wheels back and forth to the Goodyear

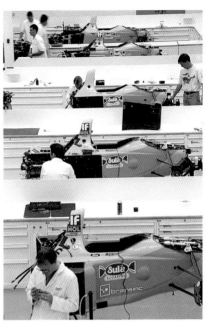

Above

The spacious, well lit environs of the race preparation department. Within the scrupulously clean and immaculately laid out pens, race and test cars are constructed

Left

A carbon fibre composite undertray is prepared for loading into one of three giant vacuum ovens known as autoclaves. Once secured within, it will be baked at between 125 and 175°C for 1 to 2 hours until cured. Originally developed for the military aerospace industry, carbon fibre composites are now extensively used in Formula One. The material provides twice as much rigidity as aluminium, but for less weight. Consequently most panels, including monocoque and aerofoils, are now constructed of carbon fibre

Above

The Enstone facility houses a battery of advanced, computerised milling machines of all descriptions for metallic component manufacture. However, the traditional skill of the craftsman is alive and well. Utilizing a purpose-built jig, the complicated curves of an exhaust manifold are welded into shape

Right

John Wheatley and Max Fluckiger pay careful attention to precise detail on a new, in-house manufactured, carbon fibre tub. Current monocoques are estimated capable of withstanding impacts in the order of 50g before break-up. Indeed, many shunts that drivers walk away from today may well have proved fatal ten years ago

compound. Once fitted, the tyres must be pressured correctly and then heated by means of electric blankets specially designed for the purpose. Each set of tyres is marked and numbered to ease recognition by the team and allow for inspection by officials as they check no driver is using anything other than the allocation permitted by the rules.

Then it is back to the track, the driver completing a few more laps and reporting on the effects of the changes. The process is repeated until the car is better suited to the track, the degree of improvement being so subtle that it would be lost on any driver unfamiliar with the nervous nature of a Formula 1 car when pushed to its limits.

All of this takes place during so-called free practice periods on Friday and Saturday mornings. Lap times are recorded, but they do not count towards grid positions. That is reserved for qualifying, the hour-long period when drivers put their experimentation to the test in the hope

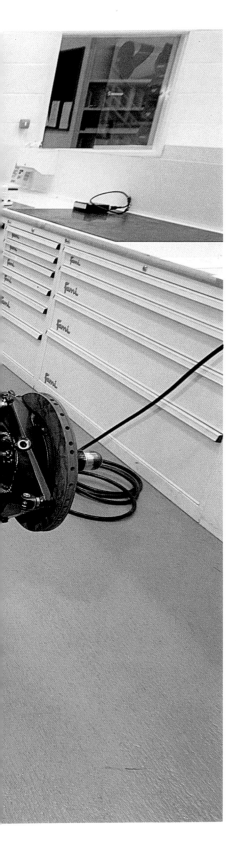

Above

With all systems checked and functioning, a custom-made nylon cover provides superficial protection for the air-freight to Canada, en route to the Montreal Grand Prix. Beneath the cover, temporary hardboard undertray and sideboards protect the largest sections of bodywork from damage, whilst the vulnerable nose-cone has been replaced by a wooden blank. The delicate rear wing is also transported separately

Left

Exposed rear flanks of the thoroughbred B193B. Ford Cosworth's V8 engine is attached directly to the rear monocoque bulkhead and is employed, together with the gearbox, as a load bearing extension of the chassis. Suspension double wishbones are in turn attached to both engine and transmission casing. The two metallic cylinders mounted above the gearbox are hydraulic actuators for the active suspension system

that they are closer to the maximum performance of the car.

The search for perfection being what it is in F1, they are rarely satisfied. Another small improvement in the handling through this corner, better traction out of that one, the ability to ride the bumps more efficiently; all of these complaints add up.

Always, it could be better. Unless, of course, the driver is fastest of all and has won pole position. Then he might admit that the car is reasonable. But rarely is it perfect.

The work goes on, even though qualifying finishes early in the afternoon. The driver's immediate task, once he has levered himself from the cockpit, is to discuss his findings, the engineers keen to extract whatever information they can while events are still fresh in the driver's

Above

An HB is given the final once over prior to shipment to Enstone. The Ford Cosworth partnership has been a front runner in motor racing engines since 1967, when the legendary Jim Clark used the outstandingly successful DFV to power his way to victory in that year's Dutch GP. For the future, Cosworth are currently developing a V12 which should provide the grunt to put them back at the top of the engine power stakes

Left

Valve recesses are milled into an alloy piston's crown at the Northampton based Cosworth factory

mind. Hovering in the background will be a posse of media people with deadlines to meet. Once the driver is seen to have finished his technical discussion, he is immediately surrounded, microphones and tape recorders thrust in his face; probing questions about a furious world which the observer, with both feet on the ground in the pit lane, cannot begin to comprehend.

In the midst of the crowd will be the team's press and public relations representative, recording the driver's thoughts. These will be transcribed and prepared in up to three languages, ready for the Benetton-Ford press release to be handed out in the media centre and faxed around the world to the headquarters of Benetton, Ford and the team's sponsors. Good news or bad, the routine is always the same.

Above left

Monte Carlo or bust. En route for the most famous and charismatic race of the calendar – the Monaco Grand Prix. We're travelling in the Ford Cosworth truck with John Cushing at the wheel. Equipment including cars, engines and spares, is transported by truck to the European based races. The smart blue-liveried Ford Motorsport truck normally travels in convoy with the pair of Benetton Scanias. Apart from the numerous spare engines, the Ford rig is also kitted out with hi-tec telemetry for the engine management system

Left

The narrow winding roads of downtown Monaco demand utmost concentration from the truck drivers. We arrived at the principality in convoy with a number of other teams transporters – a total of perhaps a dozen or so trucks. Watching these leviathans carefully negotiate the town centre was an entertainment in itself

Above

The Monaco scenery lends a suitable backdrop as Dave 'Yosser' Hughes, truckie and Patrese tyre man, unloads the T-car from the top tier of his artic. Two externally identical Benetton Scanias make the journey to each of the European races. One of the trucks, the example driven by Yoss and his mate Martin Pople, carries the most precious cargo of all – the race cars themselves. That's the three cars plus a spare chassis in case of a major shunt. The other truck, with Jon Harriss and Kristan de Groot aboard, carries all the ancillary equipment including a vast array of tools and spares. It is also fitted with a small workshop, featuring lathe, drill and grinder etc, for those necessary little jobs. As they say 'everything but the kitchen sink'. Actually now you mention it...

FORMULA ONE TECHNICAL CENTRE
FORMULA ONE TECHNICAL CENTRE

Meanwhile, the driver will have crossed the paddock to the team's motor home. (At 'flyaway' races, the management base themselves in temporary offices erected at the back of the garage, or in portacabins placed in the paddock.) The motorhome provides air-conditioned comfort and hush; a plush sanctuary in the midst of the stifling hurly-burly of the paddock.

But there is little time to relax. The motor home crew – usually a husband and wife team – will have already served lunch to sponsors and their guests, these motorised caterers working miracles from a tiny kitchen tucked downstairs in the double-deck bus.

Now it is the turn of the team management. Designers, engineers and drivers will usually have a working lunch inside the motor home as they debate the day's findings and discuss ways of making the car go quicker still.

These debriefs can take an hour and more as every aspect of the car's performance is examined in minute detail. When you are working in millimetres and talking fractions of a second, nothing is left to chance, nothing is overlooked.

The driver is then free to deal with lengthy interviews, consult with his manager, carry out sponsorship engagements or, if he is lucky, get away for a round of golf or a game of tennis. Sometimes, there is the opportunity to combine business with pleasure as drivers take part in a competition – perhaps a soccer match or a cycle race – backed by the team's sponsor.

By mid-afternoon, the public relations people will be hard at work, massaging whatever aspect of their operation is central to the commercial life blood of the team. In the case of Benetton Formula, the fashion business and Grand Prix racing make ideal bedfellows. The sleek shape of a Formula 1 car is the perfect if unusual backdrop for a modelling picture shoot. Sometimes the driver, looking strangely awkward for once, is included. The resulting photograph, when published on the glossy paper of some quality magazine, encourages the thought that the driver's life is an endless round of glamour and beautiful women.

What the picture does not show is the sweat and toil in the background as the mechanics go about their pre-race routine. They will have received a job list, drawn up by the chief mechanic and based on the

John Cushing jealously protects his territory from the poaching Pople. Mind you in that hot afternoon sun a cool soaking might be rather pleasant. The trucks, together with motorhome, are usually the first to arrive at a race venue. After cleaning the vehicles, (you soon realise that in F1, everything has to be spotless and just so – it's all part of the sponsor cultivating image) the truckie's next task is to set up the garages and lay out the benches, tools and equipment, in readiness for the mechanics arrival

Above

Suitably kitted out in shades (well they are 'Killer Loops' part of the Benetton Sportsystem) Yoss checks the pressures of Riccardo's tyres, in preparation for Saturday's practice session. The designation D4970 that is visible on the paper label signifies a softer C compound rubber, more suited to the tight and twisty curves of the street circuit

Left

The first day of practice/qualifying at Monaco proves to be very wet, and Riccardo's race shoes are mopped dry prior to entering the cockpit. Wet soles could all too easily slip off accelerator or brake pedal with potentially disastrous results. Behind the car Tom Walkinshaw, Rory Byrne, Frank Dernie, Gordon Message and Christian Silk huddle in a tactical briefing

outcome of the earlier debrief. The alterations will be added to the routine checks as the car is stripped and examined, the mechanics working with delicate care on an intricate car which, paradoxically, will endure more mechanical stress and severe punishment in an hour than your road car would experience in a life-time.

There will be a break at around 7 pm for dinner at the motor home. Then it's straight back to the garage. On a good night, the mechanics will be finished by 9 pm. On a bad one, there may be just a few hours' sleep before the early morning departure from the hotel and another day of the same.

Left

The yellow smudge is Schumacher, as a pit board is offered out with qualifying information. Being a street circuit the race facilities at Monaco are very much temporary and 'make-do'. For the teams it is a location of contrasts. Everyone wants to be there because of the unique atmosphere, but the operating conditions, particularly during bad weather, are awkward and primitive

Above

Chief Mechanic, Mick Ainsley-Cowlishaw monitors the proceedings via the airwaves. All mechanics and engineers are kitted out with head-sets, for use during the track sessions that conspire to make communications rather difficult. Radio also of course enables two-way contact with the drivers whilst on track

Left

For the spectator and photographer, Monaco just has to be the Grand Prix of the year. The beautiful and varied scenery and dynamic nature of the track, combine to make it a truly awesome spectacle. As the cars round the chicane, the most efficient 'racing line' has become exposed by a dark build up of rubber on the tarmac surface

Above

Riccardo prepares to round Loews hairpin during the Saturday qualifying period. Race weekends traditionally consist of three days, Friday to Sunday. Monaco of course just has to be a little different. Here the first day of practice/ qualifying is on Thursday with Friday as a rest day. The mechanics still have to work but it does spread the load a little

Yet the mechanics would have it no other way. It beats the mundane routine of a nine-to-five job and, besides, there is the chance to play an active part in the outcome of the race when they bring their well rehearsed and dramatically efficient tyre-changing routine into operation.

Under normal circumstances, the mechanics would expect each car to stop at least once for fresh rubber. In the event of changing weather conditions, however, there can be several switches between wet and dry-weather tyres. On such high-stress occasions, races can be lost by a fumbled wheel nut. The pressure is immense.

There is little time for the mechanics to see the sights, the routine being airport, circuit, hotel, circuit, hotel, until it is time, a few days later, to head for the flight home. But there is a strong sense of camaraderie. Even though mechanics from rival teams know they are out to beat each other, there is an unspoken feeling of working for the same exclusive club.

And yet there is little time to socialise together. One of the few exceptions is the Canadian Grand Prix where a former Olympic rowing lake at the back of the paddock provides the perfect location for the annual F1 raft race.

The rules are as simple as the methods of construction. The raft must be cobbled together from material found in the paddock; a perfect exercise for the ingenuity which must be part of any racing mechanic's

Above

The narrow, winding pit lane at Monaco doesn't possess actual garages, just shelters that are too small to accommodate the cars. Consequently they are wheeled to the pit area early in the morning together with all necessary tools and spares. At the end of the final track session the whole lot is manhandled the few hundred yards back to the harbour side paddock. Here, beneath the awning, all major engineering work is undertaken. Not the ideal setup, but the mechanics are able to adapt

Left

Back under the awning following final qualifying, Rory Byrne issues the mechanics, the unsung heroes of F1, with their job lists. Rory is Chief Designer at Benetton and has been working in the motor racing industry since 1972. For most of that time he was involved with various Toleman-backed formulae and his car designs brought results right from the word go. Working closely with Ross Brawn, it is largely Rory's pen that has made the ever more successful Benetton F1 cars what they are today

trade. The results vary from the resourceful to the hilarious, the audience at the water's edge showing their encouragement by hurling abuse and raw eggs in equal amounts. Most of the drivers are there to witness the fun.

The relationship between the man in the cockpit and those working on his car is founded on trust. There is nothing a mechanic appreciates more than to have a driver step into the car that has been slaved over for hours on end and watch him put the thing on its ear. That's what the car is there for and, after a back-breaking effort, the mechanic wants to see the product of his labours used. And, if the driver damages the car occasionally, well, so be it. At least he was trying hard.

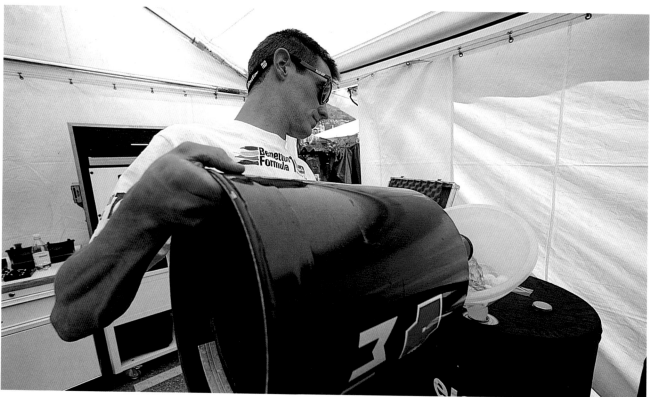

Above left
Having rebuilt the gearbox, Jake and Bob refit the rear casing and wing mount. Nowadays most teams employ semi-auto gearboxes, to permit quicker gear changing and without taking a hand from the steering wheel, particularly undesirable when accelerating forcefully through corners. The driver pre-selects the gear and then initiates the change by squeezing a paddle on the steering wheel

Left
Martin Pople, when not driving a truck, doubles as the fuel man, issuing and retrieving the Elf Minol motion lotion as required. In keeping with most things Fl, the fuel man's job is an exact science and at any time, Martin knows precisely how much fuel is in each car. Fuel weight can make a big difference to car handling and performance so, when evaluating setup, this

information is vital. Although Fl fuel must fall within the maximum octane rating available on the forecourt, the similarity ends there. Continued extensive research combined with high transportation costs makes this very expensive petrol indeed. In addition, Elf Minol supply Benetton Ford with oil designed to perform at the extreme engine and gearbox speeds and temperatures encountered in Fl

Above
The mechanics attend to his car as Michael performs a spot of engineering work of his own on the newly acquired 'chopper' motor bike. Apparently its exhaust note wasn't quite loud enough for his liking. Michael, who adores the atmosphere of Monaco is now a resident, having bought an apartment here with his girlfriend Corina. Situated in Fontvieille, it is not too far from a property owned by a certain Brazilian named Ayrton Senna

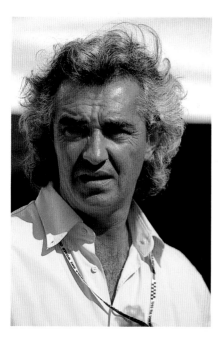

Left

The Boss. The Italian Flavio Briatore first became involved with the United Colors of Benetton after being requested by Luciano Benetton to set up a chain of shops in America. Following the successful outcome of this venture he was offered an opportunity to take a look at Benetton's FI involvement, with the object of leading the team on to bigger and better things. Since joining in 1989, his cool business sense and firm grip has indeed projected the team towards the top, and there seems little doubt that, under Flavio's command, Benetton will continue towards their goal – number one in the World Championship

Below

Sunday morning and the boys are up with the sparrows. Having uncovered the cars they manhandle them past La Rascasse, from the paddock en route to the pit area

But, more than that, it is a public expression of the driver's faith in the handiwork of his mechanics and the creative skills of his designers and engineers. When a mechanic removes grit from the soles of the driver's flameproof boots (to avoid his feet slipping from the pedals) and then straps the driver to his seat (a task made impossible for the driver to perform by the tight confines of the cockpit), it is an unspoken thought that a mistake by either side in this dangerous game can bring serious consequences.

But that is usually submerged by the surging belief that today's race will go their way. All the top teams feel the same. Grand Prix racing thrives on such incurable optimism. The atmosphere before the start is one of rampant expectation in the moments before a thrilling and dramatically cacophonous contest.

Drivers keep themselves to themselves on the grid. Some stay in their cars, helmets in place, their minds focused entirely on the race ahead. Others need to kill the time by wandering round the car, answering bland questions with automatic responses which require no distracting thought.

For the crowd in the grandstand opposite, this is one of the few chances they get to see their heroes at reasonably close quarters. The advent of a parade lap by the drivers on race morning has helped. But

Above

Flav has an informal chat with FIA (Federation Internationale de l' Automobile) president Max Mosley. As Benetton have become an increasing force within Formula One, so also has Briatore's voice become respected and his ideas and opinions carry weight. Is Flavio committed to winning the World Championship? Well, Michael Schumacher has signed up for three years. Watch this space

Right

The gearbox is in bits again on Riccardo's car. It maybe just a precautionary check, a change of ratios or perhaps something more serious. All is relatively tranquil in the Monaco pit lane at present, but it won't be long before all hell breaks loose. Any pit lane, but particularly the narrow Monaco example, can be an extremely dangerous place for the unwary, as cars rush in and out at high speed

smiles and bonhomie are not so evident as they prepare for the start.

The atmosphere on the starting grid is highly charged; the feeling being that, after two days of hype, this is the Real Thing. Even though practice and qualifying has perhaps indicated that rivals are in better shape, everyone knows that the variables and outside influences presented during a 200-mile race can wreck the best-laid plans. Luck plays a major part.

At Monaco in 1993, Benetton Formula appeared to have the race in their pocket. Michael Schumacher was unstoppable, the multi-coloured car pulling out a 15-second lead. Despite the dramatic sense of occasion unique to Monte Carlo, Schumacher was unflustered, his lines impeccable as he led the Monaco Grand Prix for the first time.

But hard-won experience has taught everyone in the pit lane that a

Above

Final adjustments are made as Willi Weber, Michael's entrepreneurial manager and mentor, confidently gives the V for victory signal. Optimism within the Benetton camp was high. For the first time they were running the B193B fitted with new traction control and all was functioning well. During the practice sessions Michael had established that the traction control system benefited lap times by 1.2 seconds – an eternity in F1. Willi's confidence in his protege was, but for an unfortunate twist of fate, to be fully vindicated

Above right

Riccardo prepares to exit the pit lane, lap the track and take up his position on the grid, as behind him Johnny Herbert rushes past in his Lotus. Riccardo was still having some problems settling in with the Benetton car and, on this occasion could only qualify a disappointing ninth on the grid

Right

The 24-year-old Schumacher, however, had stormed through his qualifying sessions, claiming a highly justified second position to Alain Prost. With Senna and Hill immediately behind him, a good launch off the grid will be essential. Kenny stands by the pneumatic starter as final checks are made to the Ford Cosworth engine. Stern faces belie the optimism felt here and are more a product of tension and nervousness than of worry

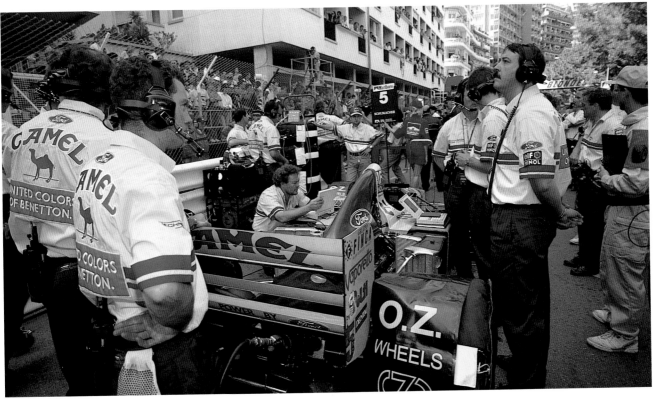

race is not over until the chequered flag falls at the end of the last lap. Thirty-two laps into the race and a hydraulic seal failed. It was a minor fault with major repercussions.

Smoke poured from the back of the car as fluid leaked onto the hot engine, the Benetton staggering as far as the hairpin outside the Loews Hotel. There, Schumacher's race reached an ignominious conclusion as marshals sprayed the car in fire extinguisher foam. The jib of a crane leaned over and this once svelte racing car took on an embarrassingly cumbersome appearance as it was winched awkwardly into the air and dumped out of sight, behind a barrier.

The rest, meanwhile, raced on without so much as a moment's sympathy for Schumacher and his crew.

During a race, the pit lane runs on neat, unrefined adrenalin. Only

Left
With the underside of his car riding just millimetres above the road, Patrese's undertray scrapes the uneven and abrasive surface in a shower of sparks as he blasts down the hill towards Mirabeau. During race week the whole circuit around Monaco sprouts protective steel Armco barriers

Above
With an established lead, thoughts of victory infiltrate the Benetton camp as Michael rounds Mirabeau, and heads down towards the famous Loews hairpin. But the Monaco Grand Prix is 78 laps and nearly two hours in duration, so there's still a long way to go

with confirmation of your car's retirement does the pulse switch from overdrive to idle and a feeling of weariness suddenly overwhelms everything else. Raw nerves are exposed in an eruption of frustration. All that work – all those hopes – and absolutely nothing to show for it. Who, in 10 year's time, will remember that your car led for 30 laps? The fact is that it didn't lead the most important lap of all; the last one.

For the winners, the sense of euphoria is immense. The mechanics finally abandon their posts in the pit lane – the fear of that unscheduled, last-minute puncture or tyre change now gone – and line the pit wall, there to wave their man home and witness the glorious sight of their car sweeping under the chequered flag. The standing around and waiting is over. All that sweat and hardship has been totally justified.

Above

Screaming down from Casino Square towards Mirabeau, Michael's B193B passes the infamous Tip Top bar, an establishment renowned for its hospitality during race week. Apparently members of the Benetton team occasionally darken the Tip Top's doors

Right

A car's aerodynamic set-up for a given circuit always involves a compromise between the slow bends and the fast straights. Moveable aerodynamic devices are not permitted in FI and consequently both front and rear wings must be fixed at a given value, an established optimum angle of attack (AOA). Too much wing produces inefficient drag, slowing the car down on the straight but providing the added loading permitting higher cornering speeds. Conversely, less wing creates less drag. The ideal (but illegal) solution would be to decrease wing AOA on the straights and then increase it again as required through the bends

Above

Although Monaco is not one of the fastest circuits on the calendar, its bends, uneven surface and close proximity of unforgiving steel barriers, combine to make it one of the most challenging. Sitting at home in the armchair in front of the TV, one really cannot get a true impression of the acceleration and speeds these cars attain. To get a real impression, one that will stick in the memory, save up for a trip to Monaco where the cars rocket past, just inches (and sometimes millimetres) away from the armco at speeds in excess of 180mph. In this picture Michael is running with a 'double decker' rear wing combination, devised to exploit a loophole in the '93 rule reducing wing height from 100 to 95 centimetres. The rule was devised to reduce wing effectiveness and therefore cornering speeds. However only parts behind the rear axle are considered as 'rear wing' with those in front come under 'overall height', with the original 100 centimetre rule applying. The forward wing section could therefore be mounted higher, in a cleaner and more effective airflow

Right

Riccardo rounds Loews, an acute 180° reversal of direction, which in Grand Prix terms is as famous as Monaco itself. Highly prominent on the sidepod is the name Prince, a tennis equipment manufacturer and member of the universal Benetton Sportsystem. Also visible is the front air deflector plate, the curved panel just to the rear of the front wheels. From an original concept by McLaren, this plate is designed to separate the dirty turbulent air generated around the front wheels, deflecting it away from the radiator air intakes built into the front of the sidepods. A gap exists between the inboard edge of the plate and the nose section and through here cleaner boundary layer air is channelled into the radiators. A secondary benefit is the slight increase in downforce afforded by evacuating the disturbed air

Above

Michael leans his head into the turn to help counter the lateral g-force loading. Particularly on multi-corner, high speed tracks the effect of cornering g-forces on the neck muscles can be telling. Current state-of-the-art carbon fibre racing helmets, such as the Bell example worn by Schumacher, are both ultra-light and ultra-thin. This helps to minimise the stresses by reducing both weight and height (and therefore c of g). Most racing drivers, if not in the cockpit regularly, exercise their neck muscles with weights, in anticipation of the high lateral g-forces encountered

Left

Disaster strikes the unfortunate Schumacher. Flames pour from the rear of his car as he comes through Mirabeau for the 33rd time, still currently in the lead...

The thought that you might win, deliberately suppressed for the past two hours, now explodes in sheer, untrammelled delight. This is what it's all about. There is time briefly to join the jostling throng under the podium and salute the first three home as the trophies are presented and the champagne sprayed.

Then it's back to the garage and the task of packing up. When you've won, it's the work of a moment. When you've suffered failure, each item seems to weigh twice as much as before.

The cars, meanwhile, are sitting silently in parc ferme, the sealed off area in which the final technical inspection takes place. Wings are measured, engines checked. The cars, streaked in oil and layered with rubber and grime, look battle-worn. But somehow that seems right at the finish of a climactic weekend. Tyres, once hot and sticky, are peppered with gravel and litter picked up as the drivers finally left the clean racing

Above

... but alas, not for much longer. All hopes of Benetton's first victory in '93 go up in smoke as Michael's car grinds to a spectacular halt with hydraulic problems. Whilst he evacuates the cockpit in double quick time, the ever efficient marshalls engulf the rear of his car in foam

Left

Although the B193B is on the outside of Loews off the racing line, it's in a dangerous position and is quickly hoisted up off the track, much to the interest of guests of Loews Hotel. The Monaco Grand Prix had promised so much for the young German and for the dedicated and hard working Benetton team. Unfortunately, soon after Michael had succumbed to Murphy's Law, so Riccardo running in sixth position, lost his engine on lap 54, ironically at Mirabeau and only a couple of hundred yards from his team mate. Ayrton Senna in the red and white Marlboro McLaren, inherited the lead and maintained it for the culmination – his sixth victory at Monaco and a new record, one more than the legendary Graham Hill

Below

Back at the paddock, one thing's for sure, all that foam won't have helped the precision engineered £70,000 engine... better wash it off

line they had been religiously following while the race was in progress.

In some cases, air ducts filled with gravel bear witness to unplanned deviations from the track. But if no harm is done, that will be the subject of an amusing anecdote as the driver peels of his sweat-soaked overalls and recalls how he went to the edge but survived to tell the tale. There is just time for a shower, a quick word with the press, and then off to the airport.

Most leave by helicopter, the better to avoid the traffic jams which are part of the post-race hours at any Grand Prix. Some have already departed by the time their wrecked or broken cars are returned to the paddock on the back of a pick-up truck.

This can be the final irony for the losers. While the winning team share champagne and clean down their otherwise unmarked cars in the garage next door, the mood within your beleaguered enclosure is not helped by the sight of a once-pristine car being returned in component form, most of it covered in the thick, white dust of fire extinguisher foam.

The front doors of the garage are firmly shut. But, as the late

For all the world resembling four blocks of sticky black liquorice, the tyres from Riccardo's car demonstrate the ability of the soft rubber compound to pick up any old rubbish in their path

Often taken for granted in their everyday road use – not so Goodyear's Eagle Fl racing tyres. Costing $600 per corner, for those teams unfortunate enough to have to buy them (some of the top teams are supplied gratis in exchange for evaluation data), the modern racing tyre rides both the cutting edge of tyre technology and of grip. Here Dave Morris, a member of the fifteen-strong Goodyear Racing Grand Prix contingent, tests the balance of a freshly mounted dry weather 'slick'

A fifteen inch wide rear Eagle is removed from its rim. In theory the number of tyres used at each and every Grand Prix total 728, (26 cars x 4 tyres x 7 sets). However in order to ensure sufficient stocks of both slicks and wets Goodyear normally transport nearly 2,000 examples to each race. Air pressures in these racing tyres are critical and for optimum performance work in a narrow +/− 1 to 2 psi bracket. Average pressures are 12½ psi front and 10½ rear (cold) which, when heated by friction with the track to the correct operating temperature, expands to 20-21 psi front and 18-19 rear

Above

An orderly row of OZ Racing magnesium hubs await mating with their rubber counterparts. In essence there are two types of racing tyres, slicks and wets. Slicks, for use in dry conditions, have completely smooth tread surfaces, intended to permit the maximum amount of rubber to contact the road for optimum grip. Such tyres in rainy conditions would be useless, so 'wets' in contrast have channels cut into them to permit the evacuation of water, thus preventing aquaplaning

afternoon sunshine begins to ease back from a punishing glare, local F1 fans press their faces against the glass and grab their last chance for another year to steal a glance at the sport and its players.

Press releases are prepared; technicians examine the computer printouts; the motor home crew pack away awnings, tables, chairs, soft drinks and coffee machines. For the winning team, all of this is delayed by the surging crowd of well-wishers.

What they see is but the tip of the iceberg. They fete the man who pressed the throttle on behalf of a million-dollar industry.

For the majority of teams, it is time to leave, get away from this place. Forget today's bad luck. There is another race to think about in a fortnight's time. Another chance to go through it all again. Another chance to win.

Above

Following any track sessions or races the Goodyear enclosure becomes a hive of activity with countless tyres being removed or replaced. Teams are limited to seven sets of dry tyres per car, per race weekend. These come in four principle rubber compounds A, B, C and D, with A being the hardest and D the softest. As with the general car set-up, when selecting compounds previous knowledge and experience is a great benefit. The practice sessions provide an opportunity to confirm choice and, following each session, the Goodyear engineers are to be found wandering the garages gathering data for use by the teams. Generally the harder compounds are run in hotter conditions, helping the tyres to attain their optimum working temperatures. Track surface also has to be included in the equation however. If very rough, a harder compound to prevent undue wear might be desirable

Right

A set of 'C' compound tyres (identified by the code D4970) await use. The stencil painted figures are the tyre's individual scrutineer numbers, applied to ensure that each driver does not exceed his own personal allocation. As soon as the cars enter the garages at the end of a session, Goodyear engineers measure the tyre temperatures and wear. The running temperatures, pressures and wear rate of a tyre can reveal, to the knowledgable, a considerable amount of information regarding car set-up. Development information acquired through Goodyear's involvement in FI is channelled back into the production of road tyres. In effect the benefit is split 50/50 between development and publicity

Left
Dave Redding and Bob Bushell look on as Riccardo checks the cockpit fit

Above
At the same time, a similar discussion is going on next door, with Michael suggesting some possible minor alterations. In the quest for the driver to become 'as one' with his car, it is vital that the seat and cockpit in general are absolutely comfortable. To a degree this has to be a compromise with the narrow cockpit width desirable for aerodynamic efficiency. But if the fit of driver to seat, steering wheel and pedals isn't perfect, then performance will be lost due to discomfort, tiredness and cramp

Above

In the paddock area behind the garages, Patrizia Spinelli points out a target of interest to Michael Schumacher. Patrizia is in charge of press and public relations for Benetton Formula, her main objective being to attract non-specialist media interest. In particular this means from the high circulation, international lifestyle magazines, ones who may take an interest because of the glamour of F1 or Benetton's involvement in fashion. The more exposure Benetton and their sponsors are given from participating in Formula One, the better

Left

A parade of multi-coloured bodywork festoons the pit lane at Circuit Gilles Villeneuve, Montreal, location for the Canadian Grand Prix. The circuit is actually situated on Notre Dame, an island in the St Lawrence river

Above

Benetton's happy Operations Manager Joan Villadelprat leads a quartet of laughter at Montreal. It seems that at Benetton, the people genuinely enjoy themselves and make the most of the lifestyle and special opportunities presented them. The essence of a good Formula One crew is teamwork and at Benetton this is gelled by a genuine friendship and will to win

Left

Issue number two of the 'Benetton Formula Magazine' is fresh off the press for the Canadian Grand Prix. Published in English and Italian, BFM offers the reader an unusual and sometimes light-hearted look at Fl, presenting a balanced mix of technical information and general interest articles

Above

Michael takes a moment out to discuss tactics with his manager Willi Weber. An ex
driver himself, Willi discovered 'FI's next Senna' and has since then guided his
meteoric career. Indeed, it was Willi who first opened the door for Michael by getting
him a drive at Jordan. Now Schumacher is a major celebrity, particularly in Germany,
with media interest and commercial opportunities to match. At the Grand Prix, Weber
helps take the pressure from his young protege by time-managing Michael's media
and sponsor engagements. He ensures that the necessary commitments are kept but
not to the detriment of Michael's race preparation. Michael Schumacher has
committed to three more seasons with the team: 'If it all comes together, we have a
really good opportunity to be World Champions. And that's why I'm staying'

Left

Benetton's entry into the annual Montreal mechanics' raft race receives its final pre-
race shake down. The venue for this spectacular event is Ile Notre Dame's Olympic
rowing basin, situated to the rear of the pits and paddock area. The rafts are
constructed during race week from just about anything that will float, and vary
dramatically in their seriousness and sophistication

Above

It's 07:30 race day and the vital technique of pitstop is given a final polish. The practice usually commences with a couple of static car wheel changes and then, to make things a little more realistic, the car is pushed in, to arrive in motion

Above right

No sooner has the 'driver' stamped on the brakes than the front and rear jack-men lift the car, during which time the three men in each corner spring into action. One operates the pneumatic gun, one takes the wheel off and the other puts on. With two more men who clear any debris from the radiator ducts and the chief mechanic, (Mick, with the 'Brakes On' board) this makes a total pit crew of seventeen

Right

In addition to the tyres, the other item that occasionally needs to be changed is the vulnerable nose section. Here Mick Ainsley-Cowlishaw confers with Paul Seaby about a slight problem in the nose changing procedure

Left

Taking a break before the action begins …

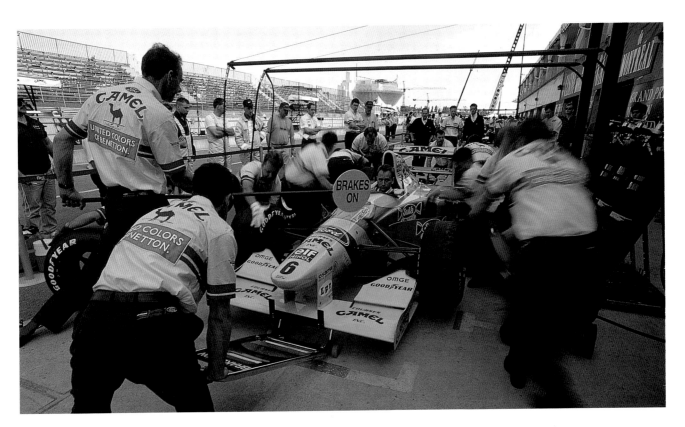

Above

Pierre Vangin of Bell Helmets lends his absent Arai counterpart a little support. Pierre attends all sixteen Grands Prix, servicing each F1 user of Bell products, not just Schumacher. He is also responsible for the beautiful custom paintwork that adorns Michael's carbon fibre shells – and there's a new one for each race. In total, with his other Bell customers, Pierre paints around 250 helmets per year

Right

Sets of Goodyear Eagles are wrapped snugly and ready for use in electric blankets, to keep the rubber compounds up to temperature and thereby afford immediate grip. The blanket temperatures are set to 80°C, whilst the optimum tyre running temperature varies between 100 and 115°C depending, as with pressures, on car set-up, track surface and tyre compound

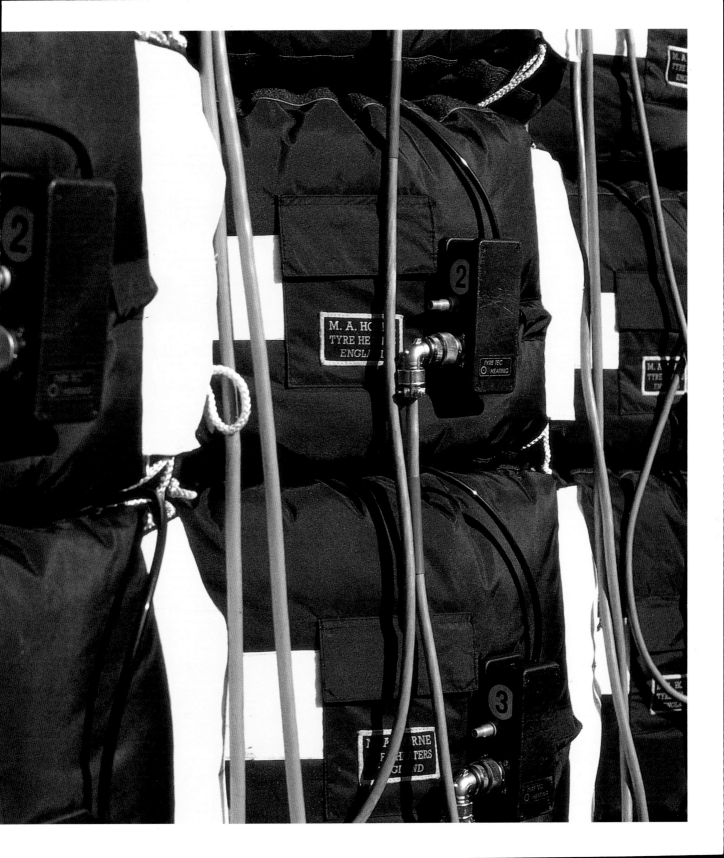

Above

The white hose fitted into the left side of
Patrese's helmet is connected to an
oxygen supply and in the event of a
crash and fire, this permits a clean air
supply whilst evacuating the car. During
the long, hot races dehydration is a
major problem, and one that is
compounded by the intense stress and
thick fire-resistant nomex uniforms.
Under extreme conditions it is possible
for drivers to sweat off two litres of fluid.
Consequently most drivers have a drink
pack fitted in the cockpit, the liquid
being sucked up via a tube inserted into
the front of the helmet

Right

One of Pierre Vangin's many creations

Above
Having already despatched Jean Alesi in one scarlet Ferrari, Schumacher sets his sights upon the other, driven by Gerhard Berger on lap 6, to claim fourth position...

Right
... and having passed Berger has the opportunity (but probably not the time) to watch himself on the giant circuit monitor, as the Ferrari's on-board camera captures the action

Above left
The pit crew have a chance to put into practice their training at changing nose-cones on lap 45 when Riccardo spins, breaking off a front wing section, and has to stop for a replacement

Left
Sadly the Italian wasn't to last much longer, retiring with cramp seven laps later. Perhaps his cockpit fit wasn't right after all

Above
Schumacher as ever performs well under pressure and makes it all look so very easy. The characteristic Ross Brawn designed 'sharks nose' of the Benetton cars may not be too aesthetically pleasing but, from an aerodynamic point of view, it is efficient. The system of suspending the front wing beneath the nose on narrow struts permits the entire length of the aerofoil surface to be effective in producing downforce

Above

As the Canadian Grand Prix draws to a close Schumacher's car exhibits tell-tale signs of a long and hard race. The front surfaces together with his crash helmet are covered in oily dirt. Michael had driven a storming race in challenging conditions to claim second place behind Alain Prost. To withstand the rigours of a Grand Prix, drivers have to be in peak physical condition. The stress of the race is extreme with drivers pulse rates averaging between 180 and 200, comparing dramatically with a normal rate of 60 to 75

Right

After taking the flag, the Benetton is pushed into parc-ferme together with the cars of Prost and Hill, ready for the post race scrutineering to begin. Michael, Alain and Damon will already be making their way, via the TV booth for a quick live interview, to the rostrum for the traditional victory celebrations

Above

Looks like a Goodyear engineer has been here. Excess rubber has been scraped off from around the tread measuring indents, permitting a record of Michael's race tyre wear. The surface of the tyre has regular recesses across the smooth tread to permit such evaluation. These tyres must withstand cornering forces of 4 to 6 g and massive downloads generated by the car's aerodynamics. In addition, the centifugal forces are tremendous, subjecting the tread face to 2,500 g at 200mph; which equates to a force of over 25,000 lbs

Left

Dripping wet following the sticky champagne fight, the effervescent Schumacher savours every second. In 38 Grands Prix, he scored points in 23 up to the end of the 1993 season, a remarkable record of consistency, and never with the fastest machinery. There will be many more such scenes to come

TIMEKEEPING: FORMULA ONE'S YARDSTICK

In the world of Grand Prix an important and necessary task, one that is often taken for granted, is timekeeping. Without highly accurate and reliable timekeeping, particularly during qualifying, grid positions would be impossible to quantify.

This operation is performed by TAG Heuer of Switzerland, a company renowned the world over for their high quality, precision sports watches. In order to perform their alloted task to the standard required in Formula One, TAG Heuer transport over one hundred containers of equipment, including 130 monitors, to each and every race. Sixteen technicians ensure that all the kit performs as planned.

In Formula One there is no room for error and this applies where timing is concerned. Often during the Grand Prix itself the position differential between race cars is discernible to the naked eye, even though it may be just a matter of centimetres. However, the situation is quite different during the practice and qualifying sessions, when each driver performs his laps individually. Then there is no visual basis for comparison and all laps completed by all drivers have to be logged accurately to determine their positions on the starting grid. At certain circuits where overtaking is difficult – Monaco is a case in point – a good grid position will often make all the difference. The slightest error in timekeeping could thus benefit or penalise the chances of a driver.

Timing twenty-six cars simultaneously, all of which can clock up more than 300 km/h, is a major challenge. The timekeeping system installed for each Grand Prix must be absolutely reliable and operate faultlessly in varying climatic conditions. A breakdown in even just one system would be catastrophic.

For every lap of every car the TAG Heuer Olivetti system (Olivetti takes care of the data processing side of the operation) instantaneously processes and puts out to monitor screens an impressive array of data; best lap time so far and the lap on which it was achieved, total laps completed, average speed and top speed on the fastest stretch of the circuit.

In order to eliminate all risk of error TAG Heuer employ three autonomous timekeeping systems. The first of these is linked to a photocell installed at the finish line and measures lap time and speed of competitors each time they pass the line. The second system consists of an aerial installed on the circuit which receives a series of pulses emitted

Above right
TAG Heuer the well known Swiss sports watch manufacturer, also perform the demanding and challenging task of timekeeping at the Grands Prix. This awesome but essential undertaking requires the transportation of over 100 containers of equipment, including 130 monitors to each and every race

Right
Technicians from TAG Heuer ensure that the infra-red photocells are functioning as advertised. These will be strategically placed around the circuit to measure, in thousandths of a second, the speeds and lap times of all 26 competitors. TAG Heuer invest a substantial amount of money each year into the continued development of their precision timing systems, in order to maintain their position at the forefront of the industry

by small transmitters fitted in front of the pedal boxes on all cars. These transmitters are set to different frequencies to identify each individual car as it passes, and the lap times are recorded. The third utilises a high-definition video camera located at the start finish line. Shooting at 100 frames per second, the camera continuously records the competitors as they pass, with the timing data superimposed on each frame.

TAG Heuer invest a substantial amount of money annually into the continued development of their timing systems. In common with many other systems manufacturers, for them Formula One is the ultimate in research and development catalysts. Information acquired through TAG's involvement in the world's most prestigious and demanding sport is channelled into the development and production of their sports wrist watches. Michael Schumacher, in addition to other FI drivers, wears a TAG in his everyday life (as well as in his race car!).

Motor racing is a sport in which everything hinges on timekeeping. Indeed, it is the only factor which makes it possible – either during qualifying or testing – to monitor driver and car performance throughout sections of the track, and thereby establish where a car's potential lies, ultimately to enhance that potential. In Formula One, the chronometer is the yardstick, and there is no appeal against its verdict.

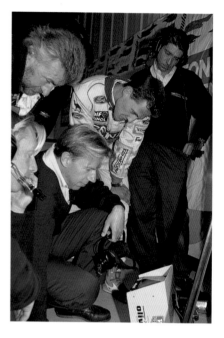

Below left
An anxious Frank Dernie looks on as Michael, strapped in and ready to scramble, switches between live camera coverage and posted lap times. With qualifying lap allowance per driver severely limited, part of the strategy in race qualifying is selecting just the right moment to hit the circuit.

Above
All eyes are focused avidly on the TAG Heuer monitor as final grid positions for the British Grand Prix are determined. Having damaged his own car Michael uses Riccardo's (and only eight of his twelve lap allowance) to ultimately claim third on the grid behind Prost and Hill

Right
Michael's flame retardant Sparco race-suit is covered with logos, all strategically positioned to maximum effect

Above
A Ferrari splashes down the Silverstone pit road as representatives of the Benetton contingent huddle beneath their awning in response to the unrelenting wind and rain. This was the first untimed practice session and neither United Colors cars were to venture out. There would be absolutely no point in risking damage to the precious race cars in these inclement conditions, when times do not apply anyway

Above
It's Friday afternoon and the rain has at last passed over to reveal some heart-warming rays of sun. The Benetton crew take advantage of the situation to push a car down the pit lane for scrutineering

Right
In order to comply with tobacco advertising regulations Camel, Benetton's title sponsor until the 1994 season, had to adopt different branding strategies for different countries. This all required an immense amount of care and preparation to ensure the correct advertising logo was used, and the same applies for the new sponsor Mild Seven. Cars, race-suits, helmets, jackets and shirts etc, all need to exhibit the correct branding; contravening the advertising regulations would be a costly error

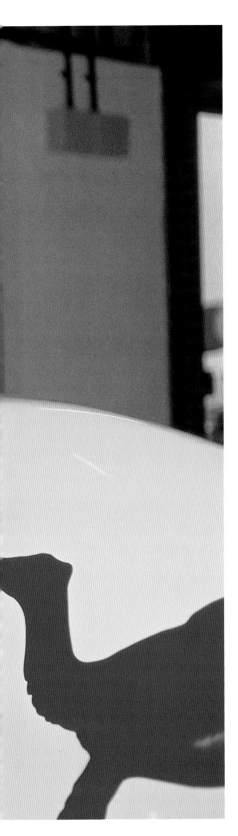

Above

Engine systems are monitored utilising a lap top computer. Much of the technology of FI was banned for 1994, with systems such as traction control and active suspension outlawed. The primary objective of this move was to make racing more exciting by attempting to close the gap between the top four teams – Williams, Benetton, McLaren and Ferrari – and thereby create more of a race for the championship

Left

A member of FOCA Communications television crew fits the 'on car' minicam housing onto the side of Michael's car. The advent of ultra small radio minicam lenses means that a camera can be fitted to just about anywhere on the car. The 'drivers eye view' mounting seen here is intended to put the viewer into the cockpit. Currently some five hundred million people in over one hundred countries watch Formula One on television and, if these figures are to be maintained, the spectacle of Grand Prix needs to be improved. From a televisual point of view, the American IndyCar series is more adventurous, with novel and enterprising use of cameras and direction

Above left

During the final qualifying session at Silverstone, Michael takes a dive into the barrier at Copse. Rules dictate that he cannot then transfer to the T-car so, as he runs back to the pits, Riccardo is instructed to condense his own session, permitting Michael sufficient time to jump in his car for the final few minutes. The pit lane marshalls wave their cautionary flags as Patrese blasts down the pit road, inbound the Benetton garage...

Left

... and once there is manhandled back into the confines of the shelter. Throughout the season the cars carry names of Benetton Sportsystem members upon their sidepods. At Silverstone, pride of place goes to Kastle, manufacturers of mountain bikes. Consisting of eleven previously independent companies, Benetton Sportsystem coordinates the various brands' marketing and distribution. Other members featured on the sidepod hoardings include Rollerblade, Prince, Nordica and Killer Loop. Total sales for the Benetton Sportsystem products in 1992 reached nearly $600 million

Above

Having arrived back at the pits, Schumacher is given a situational briefing by Technical Director Ross Brawn. Ross, who has many years of experience in F1, was invited to join Benetton Formula in July 1991 by Engineering Director Tom Walkinshaw. The design of the B192 and 193 was his responsibility in partnership with Rory Byrne, as is the forthcoming passive B194

Right

Michael plays an expensive and ultra hi-tec video game as he gets an Ayrton Senna's eye view lap of Silverstone, courtesy the TAG monitor

Below

At the end of the final session and using a car set-up different to his own, Michael has managed to relegate Ayrton to fourth place on the Silverstone grid. The TAG Heuer Olivetti timing system tells the story and the Benetton crew are not at all unhappy with its verdict...

Above

... as can be seen by the congratulatory smiles offered the affable German once back at the garage. To Michael's right is Gordon Message, Benetton's team manager. Some state that young Schumacher has an arrogant attitude but, in reality this is not so. He's often to be seen laughing and joking with members of the team and other drivers. Michael also realises (to a greater degree than some other drivers his senior) how responsible his position is, and how important his actions are, as an ambassador for Formula One, Benetton and Germany

Right

At the back of the Silverstone garages Dave Jones, better known as Reg (after the British comedian Reg Varney), prepares to make good some minor damage to a carbon fibre sidepod. Once the surface is prepared he will mix the resin and hardener, (similar to araldite glue) and then combine this with layers of carbon fibre material to consolidate the repair

Above

To help promote Kästle, Benetton organised a charity bike race, one circumnavigation of the 3.25 mile Silverstone circuit. The superfit Schumacher demolished all opposition before him to claim a comprehensive victory. Regarded as the fittest driver in Fl, Michael takes his training very seriously indeed, usually doing two hours of gym work and one hour on the bike every day. He believes that such a peak of physical fitness is virtually an essential prerequisite for success in Formula One, helping to combat the stress and tiredness encountered during a race distance, and also developing mental stamina and alertness

Above right

Benetton are a household name in the fashion industry and it is therefore perhaps no surprise that the yellow and green team frequently open their doors to fashion magazines. It's all good exposure after all. Electra from Storm model agency in London, holds still as Wendy Rowe prepares her make-up for the camera

Right

Meanwhile out back, the Ford Motorsport truck's blue coachwork seems to complement that red coat rather nicely

Far right

Electra puts on the look for Burda International, a German fashion magazine

Above

The engines live their short existence in the fast lane, each having a maximum duration of only 400km before needing a complete rebuild. That's just sufficient for the Sunday morning warm-up and race distance. The cost of a rebuild? Somewhere between twenty to forty thousand pounds, depending on degree of abuse

Left

A brand new Ford Cosworth Series VIII HB engine awaits fitting to Schumacher's car for the Sunday warm-up and race. Constructed of aluminium with a displacement of 3494cc, the Series VIII features 32 pneumatically controlled valves (four per cylinder) and double overhead camshafts, producing 730bhp at 13,500 rpm. The new Cosworth engine for 1994 promises even more, chasing after the ever dominant Renault V10

Above

Patrese's number 6 reposes peacefully in the warm sun in preparation for another pit-stop practice session. In the background representatives from The United Colors monitor their McLaren adversaries' endeavours with great interest. The four air bottles dressed in custom made black covers provide power for the pneumatic air guns, one for each corner

Opposite

The car rushes in with Schumacher at the helm and is swiftly descended upon by fourteen pairs of hands, removing and replacing the four wheels and nose-cone, all in the time it takes to read this sentence. Benetton's regular pit-stop practices, under the critical eye of Gordon Message, have paid off and they are now challenging McLaren, the previous lane champions for record time. In the last Grand Prix of the year at Adelaide, the Benetton crew achieved a lightning quick 4.81 seconds. With cumulative seconds and sometimes even fractions of a second making all the difference, it is imperative to achieve tight pit-stops and not waste valuable time with the car stationary

Above

The mischievous Dr Harry Hawelka and Herr Willi Weber conspire to perform some minor (or possibly major!) surgery upon Schumacher's racing shoes. A trained masseur, dietician and fitness conditioning expert, Harry accompanies Michael to the races, calling the shots on what food he eats in his pursuit of physical and mental excellence. Harry has turned the consumption of food into an exact science, mixing, blending and creating just the right food combinations to fuel his protege's progress

Left

The resolute Tom Walkinshaw monitors practice from the elevated vantage point of the pit wall. Tom Walkinshaw is Engineering Director of Benetton Formula and also holds a substantial financial stake in the company. An ex-racing driver himself, Tom has been heavily involved with motorsport for many years. His vast experience of both racing and business enterprises have combined to make Walkinshaw one of the most powerful and respected names in F1 today. He commands over thirty companies world-wide under the Tom Walkinshaw Racing (TWR) banner, most of which are associated with motorsport and the automotive industry

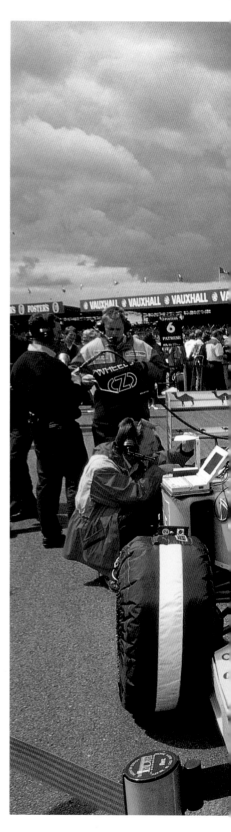

Above and left

With only minutes to go before grid clearance and the start of the race, the ever cool Michael Schumacher still finds time for that last television interview – after all it is for Fuji TV and the Japanese are Formula One fanatics. He is also relaxed enough to chat with another sporting superstar and Formula One fan, Nick Faldo

Right

The number 5 Benetton Ford, having pipped Senna to the post, takes up its now familiar third position on the grid behind the Williams' duo. Riccardo had qualified 1.8 seconds down for fifth behind Senna. As Michael confers with Ross, the mechanics make their final systems checks

Left

As Schumacher hurtles down the opening straight on lap 20, 'Gordie' Message offers out the pit-board indicating third position. Although there is a direct radio link between car and pits this is never to be relied upon and the traditional pit-board is alive and well. Although in this case no times are indicated, '-Prost' shows that the Frenchman is in front of him and '+Senna' indicates Michael is ahead of Senna

Above

However, there's happiness all round in the Benetton Ford camp with for the first time in the year, both drivers on the rostrum, Michael second and Riccardo third. The two Benetton partners douse each other in Moet in a display of unalloyed joy, as the amiable Prost contributes to the celebrations from the top step

Right

Meanwhile it's an anxious thirty minutes for Gordie and Mick who await the scrutineers thumbs-up from behind the wire fencing. Team Manager Message is another long serving member of Benetton, having joined as a mechanic during the early Toleman days

Below

In the parc-ferme Senna's Marlboro McLaren is wheeled into position as the scrutineers begin their methodical inspection

Above
The Ligier and Ferrari crews commence the cosmetic facelift operation. It's surprising just how much dirt can be picked up through the duration of a race distance, mainly consisting of oil and rubber debris off the tyres

Right
Back at the Benetton garage it's an emotional and possibly somewhat relieved Riccardo who shares his feelings with Rory Byrne and Frank Dernie, and for that matter, with just about anyone and everyone in the vicinity

Above
With trophy box on his shoulder, Mario, a long time friend and confidant, accompanies Riccardo as he attempts to make a sneaky, crowd busting getaway from Silverstone. Nice colour coded helmets!

Left
It was good to see the likeable Italian on the rostrum and to see just how much it genuinely meant to him. For once it was Patrese in the limelight and desired by the TV cameras and reporters. '93 had been a rotten season for him up to now – perhaps this would be a confidence booster and turning point. In reality, of course, it would be J J Lehto partnering Michael in 1994

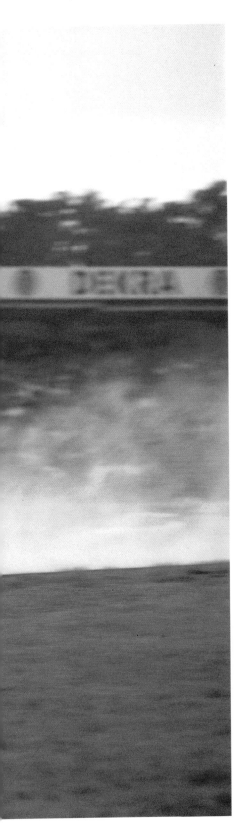

Above

To control all the technology mounted on current Formula One cars requires a high degree of input from the driver. Systems such as the fuel mixture, front and rear suspension, balance, over/understeer and degree of traction control (in 1993 anyway) could all be adjusted from in the cockpit. The two small rectangular digital screens, situated on the dash above the steering wheel, are speedometer (left) and gear selection information (right)

Left

Home is the hero and 'Michael Mania' is in full swing. Grim weather does nothing to deter the devoted fans of young Schumacher. All are keen to see their idol in action at Hockenheim in 'his' Grand Prix

Above

Michael reviews the lap times of his adversaries and awaits the command to launch from the Hockenheim garage. Over his visor he wears a removable plastic 'rip-off'. When this film gets oily and dirty, by pulling at the tab on the left he can rip off the top surface, leaving a fresh clean visor beneath

Left

Both race car and trackside are strategically adorned with sponsors' messages as Patrese enters the Motodrome amphitheatre. Sponsorship is the lifeblood of Formula One. In addition to Benetton's own investment and that of title sponsor Camel, Mild Seven (Japan Tobacco) for 1994, there are a large number of other backers, all with different degrees of exposure, dependant on size of capital or material investment. J J Lehto, for example, sports a small patch on his arm for 1994 – ' Frazer' – a Finnish chocolate company, a relatively tiny amount of sponsorship brought in by the new boy. The sponsors who pump substantial sums into teams such as Benetton are essentially looking for three returns for their money. Firstly and most obviously is television exposure, on a massive global basis. Generally speaking of course the more successful the team, the more successful the coverage attained. Second is corporate hospitality, providing an opportunity to bring guests to the races, making use of the Paddock Club and its unique atmosphere to wine, dine and influence. Thirdly, there are advertising spin-offs, using car, driver or team name to endorse a product

Left

Schumacher enters the pit road at the end of final qualifying amidst a barrage of waving flags and exploding fireworks. He will occupy third position on the grid behind the Willams duo

Top

The hero is quickly zapped back into the security of the garage

Above

Following the drivers' briefing, the drivers take part in a parade lap. Here Michael and Riccardo are chauffered around the motodrome on the back of an old Model T Ford

Above
A happy Flavio momentarily puts aside the pressures of high office, in the company of the legendary Niki Lauda

Left
In the recesses of the Benetton truck, Patrese, unhappy with his seventh grid position, has a quiet chat with Flavio Briatore (or should that be the other way round?). Behind them at the back is the small briefing room. Here the engineers and drivers will confer, discussing tactics and set-ups following each track session, to wring out as much information as possible

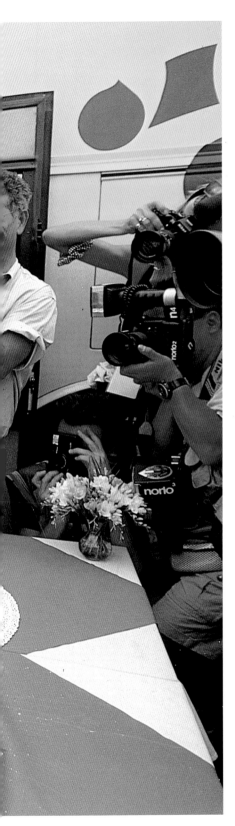

It's Riccardo's 250th Grand Prix and a jolly good cause for celebration as Flavio drenches his fellow countryman with champagne. Patrese is by far the most experienced Fl driver of all time, ahead of ex Benettonite Nelson Piquet who achieved a mere 204 starts. Riccardo made his race debut at Monaco in 1977. In his career he has won six races, taken eight pole positions and was runner up to Nigel Mansell for the 1992 World Championship

Left

The United Colors of Benetton's 'stitch' logo adorns the rubber headrest of the T-car, which was ultimately to play a very significant role in Michael's weekend

Right

Team personnel and guests mill around the Hockenheim paddock area. To the right is the orderly line of team trucks which back onto the garages and pit-lane. On the left are the motorhomes where drivers, sponsors and team members can find a place to relax and chat

Below

All part of the job. "I don't believe I'm a star. I talk to people in a normal way. I think that is the way to achieve success." (Michael Schumacher, Autosport, *January 1994)*

Above
A lull in the proceedings signifies an opportune time for the Bratwurst sausages to emerge

Left
Kenny and Max enjoy a little light entertainment via the Benetton Formula airwaves

Above

Riccardo's highly experienced eyes peer from beneath the Arai helmet. His relatively poor showing throughout the season compared with that of partner Schumacher had already led to rumours of a split between Patrese and Benetton for '94. In the high profile, high finance world of Formula One no quarter is given or expected. Ultimately Riccardo's place was claimed by Finnish driver J J Lehto, who during the 1993 season had proved his worth behind the wheel of a Sauber

Right

Tension and excitement fill the air as cars take their places on the grid, amidst the pageantry and fanfare that is Grand Prix. For Benetton in particular, the final thirty minutes had been electrifying. Following pit-lane opening at 13:30 (for a 14:00 hours start) and during the touring lap to take up his position on the grid, Michael had found an electrical problem with his car. As the minutes tick by, the decision is made to transfer to the spare car for the race – a blow considering how well his own had been set up. With only minutes to go he joins the seething entourage on the grid and prepares to manoeuvre his way through to third position at the front, where his mechanics will have to perform their final checks in double quick time

Above

The flags are waved, releasing the cars for their single formation lap, following which they will take up their respective positions for race start. Immediately the cars have evacuated the grid for the formation lap, it will be hurriedly cleared of all personnel and equipment in preparation for the start

Right

And they're off! Tension reaches fever pitch in the cockpits and the grandstands as the cars launch from the grid. At the first corner Michael has out gunned Alain Prost and occupies second position behind Damon Hill

Above
Michael Mania engulfs the Motodrome as the immense 150,000 strong crowd leave
little doubt as to who their favourite is

Above right
The exclusive Paddock Club guests are wined and dined in luxury as Schumacher
sweats it out in the cockpit for their entertainment and enjoyment.

Right
For the bulk of the German Grand Prix he was to run in third position behind Hill and
Prost. However, one man's misfortune is another's gain and, when on the penultimate
lap, the unlucky Damon Hill gets a puncture, Michael is promoted to second place,
much to the vociferous approval of the home crowd

Right

The jubilant Schumacher punches out in a display of emotion – a win here would have been unbelievable but this second place is pretty satisfying. Anyway, there's always next year. The triumphant crowd go wild as he tours the amphitheatre on the slow down lap

Above

He can't hide his happiness with the result, contrasting with the more serious and restrained composures of Prost and Blundell. Michael's beaming face has become a regular, welcome feature on the Grand Prix podiums around the world and his characteristic unbridled exhibitions of appreciation, a boon to Formula One. How sad it is that not all the drivers, who are so handsomely rewarded, put as much back into the sport that employs them as the likeable and extrovert German

At the end of 1993, Camel had taken the decision to pull out of Formula One. It wasn't long before Flavio Briatore had signed up a new multi-million dollar sponsor, Japan Tobacco Inc. Benetton unveiled the new car early, ahead of their main rivals, and stole a march on them in terms of pre-season testing. The B194 uses a spring damper system in line with the new rules, and the external shape – hardly surprisingly, in view of the ban on active suspension – is very different, an attempt to compromise and produce a car which performs well under different conditions and fuel loads without the former advantage of changing ride height

Overleaf

Jubilation finally at Estoril in Portugal. Schumacher stands upon the top step of the podium and soaks the ecstatic and grateful Briatore in Moet – this is what Grand Prix is all about. It's Benetton's only win of the season and Michael's second in his F1 career, but definitely it will not be their last